Unlocking

the Heavens

Effective Prayer Strategy

By

Ruth Shinness

Unlocking the Heavens

To obtain additional copies of this material, please write to:
Ruth Shinness-Brinduse,
2539 E 450 N
Anderson, IN 46012
Email: PrayerStrategy@juno.com
Phone (765) 643-0612 & 765-642-0623
Web: www.prayerstrategy.com

Cover Artist: Jasmine Shinness

ISBN 1-58158-021-5

Published by: Evangel Press

Dedication

To LES SHINNESS, my late husband, who loved me as Christ loved the Church and gave himself to support the dreams of my heart. He was my best friend, my prayer partner and a man of the Word. He had a sense of humor that brought fun and laughter into all our lives.

To our children, the wonderful treasures that God deposited into our home: DAVID, steadfast and faithful to follow Christ; ROGER, who has the heart to look after me in my widowhood; MOLLY, for the beauty of her spirit that reflects her love for the Lord; TOM, for the visions of his heart that are in the making.

To the memory of my parents, BEN AND MARGUERITE RODGERS, and the strength of their heritage that has come down to me. My mother was a gifted speaker and teacher, and when I get up to speak, I can't help but grin, thinking that I do it with the same "flavor." My dad never gave up his visions, even in the face of many disappointments and defeats. He came forth as a winner in his later life. I too never gave up, and I also have won.

Acknowledgments

I want to acknowledge that the Lord Jesus Himself has been the one to lead me in this most wonderful pathway. As I look back, I can see that He has woven a wonderful pattern that has brought me to this exciting place in my life. He inspired the Bible and many great books and permitted circumstances that all flowed together to shape this incredible ministry. I can now thank Him for indeed "working all things together for good." Many times, I was not aware that He was there with me in my circumstances or that anything at all was happening as I prayed. Now, I see that even the smallest incidents were part of the divine tapestry.

Contents

Foreword

These effective prayer strategies were clearly sent by the Holy Spirit to Ruth Shinness. Through her years of experience, at times Ruth missed the boat. However, she finally saw the light right before her eyes. The secret had been the Word of God all along.

This message is sent to all those saints whose prayers so often seem to bounce back off the ceiling and accomplish little, making those believers feel that it has been a waste of time to pray them. Those same saints can begin to pray prayers of faith as they believe the Word they are praying, knowing that it is the will of God. When what we pray is God's will, it *will* be accomplished.

God has destined us in these last days, these final hours of time, to pray in the end-time harvest of souls, to pray like Jesus did, with the assurance that the Father is listening and moving through our prayers. As our prayers, mixed with worship, ascend into the heavens as an incense unto the Lord, they will reach His very heart. When this happens, we who pray are changed to become more like the One who prompted our prayers. We thus come to know God more through our prayer lives.

AMEN! May God bless all those who read *Unlocking the Heavens*.

Renae Herres
Song writer, worship leader and conference teacher

Introduction

In this very exciting spiritual time in which we find ourselves living, many are asking themselves what they need to do to get into the stream of God's blessings. As they hear about the way He is blessing various men and women in diverse parts of the world, they long to be able to say, "At last, it's happening to me too"!

In recent years, God has taught me to pray in my own revival and my own ministry, and I believe we can each do it. We no longer need to wait until an angel comes down to stir the waters for us to get in. We can stir them for ourselves. God has a tailor-made revival and ministry waiting for you.

Effective Prayer Strategies is the story of how I learned to pray in my own revival and about the simple scriptural prayer skills I learned along the way that made it all possible. These strategies were tested at each juncture and proved to be effective in my own personal life.

Because they worked so well for me, I began to teach them to others. Now, many others have received their own personal revival and ministry by learning to tune up their prayer lives through these simple skills.

My prayer is that Christians everywhere will learn these simple truths that can unlock the heavens and bring to Earth the good things God has been waiting to give them.

Ruth Shinness
Anderson, Indiana

Therefore, if anyone is in Christ, he is a new crea-
tion; the old has gone, the new has come! All this
is from God, who reconciled us to himself through
Christ and gave us THE MINISTRY OF RECON-
CILIATION.   2 Corinthians 5:17-18, NIV

Chapter One

My "Stay-at-Home" Instructions

My people are destroyed for lack of knowledge.
Hosea 4:6

The start of my journey into *Effective Prayer Strategies* that would enable me to begin *Unlocking the Heavens* came in 1965 when I had an experience with the Lord that ignited a fire within me. I now set my heart to seek God, spending time reading the Bible, praying and reading good Christian books. For the next five years, I busied myself with this search and with going to prayer meetings and spiritual happenings around town. I was having a great time in God.

During those same years, however, something else was happening in my life as well. I was somehow involved in a series of small automobile accidents. They were nothing serious — a little bump here and a little scrape there. The damage was always minimal, and the accidents were never my fault. Still, I began to get the feeling that God was trying to tell me something. When I stopped long enough to listen, I could hear a small inner voice saying, "I want you to stay home."

I knew what I was hearing, but I couldn't understand it. Looking at my calendar, I couldn't see anything I could give up. Everything I was doing was important.

Aside from my spiritual activities, I ran errands for my husband Les (who owned a dental lab), I took cookies to the school, and I did the many other things a busy mother of four needed to do. What could I cut from my busy life?

This all came to a climax one ice-cold January day in 1970. My son was driving me home that day, and as he turned into our driveway, I caught sight of something out of the corner of my eye. A car had been following too closely behind us, and it was now sliding on the ice right toward my door. *Oh, no!* I thought. *Not again!* And then I felt the impact.

We were unhurt, but after I had gone into the house, a fear came upon me. It was not a bad fear, but a fear of the Lord. I knew I had to begin to make some changes in my lifestyle.

I was president of my women's fellowship, and the next day we had our monthly meeting. I stood up that day and resigned.

It wasn't enough, for still God spoke to me. As I was coming home that day in our second car, another car backed out of a driveway directly into my car's path and dented a fender. When I got home, I said, "Lord, do You have something else to say to me?"

That day, the instructions of the Lord came to my mind as they never had before. He said to me, "I want you to stay home and seek Me. Only go out when your husband goes out."

"But, Lord," I objected, "he doesn't like to shop." There was no answer, and I knew that God would work out the details of our daily lives.

He told me to be dressed and have my housework done by eight in the morning. I was to praise and worship Him from eight to nine each morning, and the rest of the day (until my son arrived home from school at two-fifteen) was to be spent in Bible study, prayer and counseling with those who were in need. I would have after school and weekends free.

Was I to become a recluse? By no means! Les and I were part of community activities, and we also enjoyed meetings that added to us spiritually. But from that moment on, I would be spending a lot more time at home, and this would continue for the next twenty-five years. If I had known all this at the time, the thought of it might have seemed rather dreary to me. But by God's grace, I enjoyed every minute of my time spent with the Lord.

I set myself to pray and read the Scriptures, and in the years to come I would usually read the Bible through at least once a year and sometimes much more. Since I could not go out, I held prayer meetings and even had a Christian bookstore in my home for part of that time. If I couldn't get out to others, I would have them come to where I was.

At first, all of this was not clear. I thought that God was just confirming my responsibility to my family, and I busied myself being a keeper at home and praying for the members of our family. It was only with the passing of time that God's plan for my life would prove to be much broader.

It might have seemed to some that I was wasting my time during those years, but I knew that I was doing something very worthwhile in His Kingdom. That is not to say that I was not severely tested. I was.

For instance, after five years of staying home and praying (primarily for my family in the early years), a serious situation arose with our son. We learned that he had begun using drugs and alcohol. When this came to light, I was devastated and felt that it represented the death of my vision. If God had told me to stay home and pray for my family, and this terrible thing had happened, I was a failure.

I had done everything I knew to do, and it apparently had not worked, and suddenly I had no idea what I should do next. Later in life, I would look back and realize that God wanted me to know that others could also give their time to prayer and the Word of God and still not receive the answer to their heartfelt needs. Like me, they would be left feeling that there must be something more.

There was something more ... much more. The next twenty years of my life became a practice session for learning prayer skills to bring forth a flow of answers that God had always planned for my life. For a long while, I did not have a clue as to what was happening in my spiritual life. It is only now, as I look back, that I can understand it all. God was teaching me so that I could teach others effective strategies for prayer. He was preparing me for *Unlocking the Heavens*.

Chapter Two

My First Prayer Skills

*I have set watchmen upon your walls, O Jerusalem,
who will never hold their peace day or night; you
who [are His servants and by your prayers] put the
Lord in remembrance [of His promises], keep not
silence, and give Him no rest until He establishes
Jerusalem and makes her a praise in the earth.*
                                    Isaiah 62:6-7, AMP

I learned my first prayer skill in a church that taught
me to pray the promises of the Word of God and claim
them as my own. I learned to pray this promise from
Isaiah, for example, in this way: *"Until He establishes [the
Shinnesses] and makes [them] a praise in the Earth."* How
often was I to remind God of His promises? *"Day and
night."* For how long? *"Until He establishe[d]"* that promise. It worked. As I declared what God's Word said, it began
to come to pass.

I thought, *If this works for the salvation of my loved one, it
will work for other things too. I have nothing to lose and every-*

13

thing to gain by trying this. So I began to search for scriptural promises that had to do with every problem I faced in life.

I bought a small three-ring notebook and wrote in it the topics for which I needed scriptural promises. For instance, I needed a healing, so, as I would read my Bible and come across scriptures having to do with healing, I would record them in the notebook.

I had a fear that embarrassed me, and nothing I did seemed to get rid of it. I found scriptures having to do with being set free from fear, and I wrote them in the notebook.

I was believing God for all my children to serve Him, so I looked for scriptures having to do with God teaching my children and cleansing their ways, etc. When I found them, I recorded them in the notebook.

Other than the special topics I was searching on, I often ran across scripture verses that just seemed to "light up" when I read them. This was God's way of saying special things to my heart. These verses, too, I recorded in the notebook.

A series of these "lighted-up" type of scriptures had to do with missions and going forth. I told the Lord that I wasn't interested in going out and preaching, but that I just wanted to see my son saved. Still, I put these scriptures in my scripture book and prayed them along with the others. Their meaning would become apparent only years later.

I wanted to be careful not to take the meaning of scriptures out of context. My guideline was to ask myself, "How has God dealt with His children in the past?" Since we are God's people, I was confident that He would deal with us in the same way. I asked myself, "What is the heart of the Father for His beloved ones?" The answers to these questions gave me freedom to use God's promises for my own life that particular day.

I was insistent in my prayers. I would say to the Lord, "If all these scriptural promises are *'yea and amen'* to us, as Your Word teaches, why don't I have them? And why don't others around me have them either?" I was not accusing God, for I was sure there was nothing wrong on His part. Something had to be wrong with my understanding of His promises or of what I needed to do to receive them.

I realized that I had much to learn about effective prayer, so when I found scriptures relating to prayer, I also wrote them in my little notebook, and I used them in my prayers.

At first, I wasn't sure exactly how to pray all these promises, so I would just read them off before the Lord. Surely He knew that I was seeking answers to the question, "What are the keys in these scriptures on prayer that will unlock Heaven's answers for me?" I was confident that He would understand and answer me.

Even with this new and exciting element in my prayer life, prayer was not always easy for me during those years. Sometimes I would grow weary and start to fall asleep. To keep myself awake and alert, I got in the habit of walking the floor as I prayed from my scripture notebook. What I was doing would probably not seem all that exciting to most people, and at times, it wasn't very exciting to me either. What kept me praying was the burden or the problem for which I was seeking an answer.

Suffering can become a friend when it drives our hearts to seek God and keeps us before Him. Paul wrote, *"That I may know him, and the power of his resurrection, and the fellowship of his sufferings"* (Philippians 3:10). As I look back on my life, I realize that without the force of suffering I would not have learned to unlock the heavens. It was with me day and night.

I couldn't pray *all* the time. I had other responsibilities too. But I would put the scripture book in my apron pocket and pray while I was stirring the food on the stove. I carried it in my purse and prayed from it as my husband drove us anywhere. If I had any spare moment, any cause for waiting somewhere any length of time, I prayed from the scriptural promises.

The notebook was by my bedside at night, and if my son was out somewhere and I was concerned about him, perhaps hearing a siren in the night, I would get up and pray God's promises over his life.

I put scripture promises up on the wall in the bathroom, by my bedroom mirror, and most everywhere else I looked. I had scriptures all over the house. My husband Les was a calligrapher and could cut out individual letters to spell out the promises. Above our davenport, we had written in large letters, *"How good and how pleasant it is for brethren to dwell together in unity! ... for there the* LORD *commanded the blessing"* (Psalm 133:1-3).

Les's grandfather helped raise him, and his prayer for his family had always been, "That the members of the family would all get along together." Surely the generations before us had sown seeds for our blessings.

Still, something was definitely missing. As I faithfully prayed, I could not feel the presence of the Lord. This caused me to wonder if my prayers were getting through. The heavens seemed to be brass.

It was only the fire of the problem that kept me going. Every trial had a plus factor: it kept me praying in a way I never would have otherwise. Surely there was much more to learn about effective prayer. Surely there was a way to begin *Unlocking the Heavens*.

Chapter Three

Answers Spring Forth

> *For God did not give us a spirit of timidity, ... but of power and of love and of calm and well-balanced mind and discipline and self-control.*
>
> 2 Timothy 1:7, AMP

Although it would take time for me to receive the answers to many of my prayers, one answer to prayer came to me quickly. This first answer came through the very first scripture I felt the Lord gave me to put in my scripture book.

I had had a weight problem for years, and try as I might, I could not seem to get victory over it. This caused me to feel defeated every day. The scripture I had recorded was this one from Paul's second letter to Timothy, and I began to pray it over and over again, as I was doing my housework, and when we went out. It wasn't long before I had gained the discipline to follow a weight-reduction program successfully. The result was that I lost fifty-five pounds, and I kept them off.

I later developed a lesson for weight loss in my *Prayer Strategy Resource Book* entitled "Perfect in God's Eyes." Since it worked for me, I was sure that it would work for others.

In the early morning hours of January 4, 1979, about four and a half years after I had begun praying the scriptures from my scripture notebook, there was a knock on our bedroom door. It was our son asking if he could come in. He wanted to get his life right with the Lord. He experienced a wonderful transformation in his life and went on to Bible college. After graduating from there, he taught music for several years at the college.

God did other miracles for me in answer to my insistent prayers. I can't say exactly when my terrible fear left me, but one day I suddenly realized it was gone.

Sometimes I learned that other things were hindering my prayers. For instance, in June of 1980, I became desperate in prayer. I had been confined to my bed for three weeks and had begun to wonder if I would survive. As I prayed about what was happening to me and why, I suddenly remembered how bothered I had been recently over something someone had done to me. I repented of those feelings, and my healing began immediately.

My insistent prayers brought a definite improvement to my health. I had been sickly much of my early life and had spent a lot of time in bed during my senior year of high school. At the end of the year, I'd undergone a thyroid operation. Since that time, I had a little more energy, but not much. It hardly seemed adequate to do my everyday tasks. I added to my prayer notebook the promise from Psalms 103:5:

> *My youth is now renewed as the eagle's, strong, over-*
> *coming and soaring.*

I regularly prayed those words by faith.

Sometime about 1983 I began to notice that I had more energy to do my work. I had made some changes in my diet several years before. I now used whole-wheat bread and avoided white flour and sugar, and this may have had something to do with it. But I was sure that there was much more. I felt new energy coursing through my body, and it hasn't left me till this day. Twenty-six years later, I am still able to accomplish more than most people I know.

Another answer to prayer concerned my husband. We women are always interested in fine-tuning our husbands, and I was no exception. On the very first page of my scripture book, I recorded scripture promises that I wanted to see fulfilled in Les.

That was a little strange, because Les was a wonderful husband. He loved the Lord, and he loved me uncondi-tionally and with enthusiasm. What more could I ask for?

Well, for one thing, I wanted him to pray with me and study the Bible with me. Was that too much to ask? But Les was busy with his dental lab.

Sometimes I would be burdened to pray for my hus-band for several days at a time. I knew that the Lord was doing something special with him. Just what it was, I wasn't sure, but I imagined that I would eventually find out.

In October of 1979, I again had a burden for several days straight to pray for Les. On the third day of my prayer, he came home and told me that he felt God was telling him to sell the lab he had built up over eighteen years and to join me at home in prayer and fasting and life in the Scriptures.

When Les gave me that wonderful news, my prayer burden immediately lifted. Now I knew what God had been burdening me for.

This was not exactly what I had in mind when I began praying for Les. The idea of him leaving the business altogether was a shocking one. How would we eat? How would we pay our bills? The thought made me feel a little insecure. But what could I say? I had prayed him into this decision. I was powerless to say anything against it.

Taking such a step was completely out of character for Les. He was not one to make rash decisions. I knew it had to be the Lord, and I rested in Him.

The sale of the lab went well, and by January 1 of that following year, Les was home. I wondered if he might change his mind about what he wanted to do with the rest of his life, but he didn't. He wanted me by his side to pray with him and study the Scriptures with him. And I wanted nothing more. What a precious time we had together during that period! We were learning together about *Unlocking the Heavens.*

Chapter Four

Another Trial, Another Revelation

Therefore I tell you, whatever you ask for in prayer,
believe that you have received it, and it will be yours.
Mark 11:24, NIV

In the late 1980s, Les gradually went blind. Then in 1991, we learned that he would have to undergo quadruple bypass surgery. This was necessary so that doctors could deal with an aneurysm in his aorta in a second surgical intervention just eight days later. During this second operation, Les suffered brain damage. When he left the hospital, he could not think clearly, speak clearly or walk without help. It was a miracle that we got him out of the hospital walking at all. There would be no more of the beautiful close fellowship and spiritual blending we had enjoyed together for the past many years.

I had come face-to-face with an entirely new problem. It seemed to be a twenty-four-hour-a-day nightmare, but it was this crisis that would lead me to yet another scriptural skill in getting answers to my prayers.

As I look back, I would have to say that most of my prayer skills were learned through devastating problems. This time, the answers would come more quickly.

When Les was praying with me, I had changed my routine to better blend with his prayer habits. Now, I decided that I would go back to praying the Scriptures as I had for so many years. There was just one problem. Our son-in-law had left the home, and it had become necessary for our daughter Molly and her four children to move into our house. Presently, she was home-schooling the children in our living room. I no longer had a quiet place to pray.

I bought an RV trailer that was parked at a local campground, and I began taking Les and going out there three or four days a week to pray. No sooner had I begun to pray than a scripture promise filled my mind. It was the promise of Mark 11:24.

Suddenly, I saw prayer in a new light. I had never believed that I actually received my answer *when* I prayed. To the contrary, I always felt that I needed the answer manifested before I could say I had it. All those years, I had been praying in unbelief.

Now, I wondered what I should do next. I had already prayed. Did that mean that God had already answered? If He had, what should I do? Should I quit praying and go home? Should I sell the RV?

I came to the conclusion that if I already had what I prayed for, then the very least I should do was thank the Lord for what I had and for the fact that I had it. I took the scriptures I had prayed and paraphrased them into prayers of thanksgiving.

Just as soon as I had asked for something, I would turn around and thank God for it. For instance, I would say "Thank You, Lord, that I now have [such and such]. I always wanted this, and now I know that I have it. I'm so grateful to You." My prayer focus now shifted more to thanksgiving and praise to God.

No sooner had I begun to pray in this way than I suddenly sensed a powerful presence of the Lord with me. This brought great joy to my heart. It was as if God was saying, "At last, someone believes that I hear them when they pray."

I had read many books by Christians who had learned to abide in the presence of the Lord, and had noted the wonderful changes that had come into their lives as a result. These were men and women like Brother Lawrence, Madame Guyon, Meister Eckhart and (from the twentieth century) Thomas Kelly and Frank Laubach.

Over time, I had written a book of poems about these people and what had happened when they came into a more intimate relationship with God. When each of them learned to abide with the Lord, his or her whole life changed. It was then that God's purposes for their lives unfolded before them.

Abiding in God's presence had been my greatest desire for many years, and I had tried to accomplish it. Somehow I always seemed to fail. Now, with this new type of prayer I had learned, I was able to come into the Lord's presence and have the great joy of fellowshipping with Him as these other believers had before me.

The presence of the Lord did not always come to me immediately or quickly, but after I had prayed for an hour or two, God's presence would come. I did not have to strive for it, but it became the natural outcome of my prayer life. As I showed God my appreciation, He made His presence known to me.

After a while, His presence came much more easily. As soon as I would start to pray the Scriptures, He was there. It reminded me of the Lord's promise revealed to John:

> *I will come in and fellowship with him and he with me.*   Revelation 3:20, TLB

Several months after I had started praying in the RV, I took Les and flew to Portland, Oregon, one day to visit one of our sons (who was serving on staff at a church there). When he picked us up at the airport, he said, "Mom and Dad, the strangest thing has been happening to us. Money has been coming in to us in a most unusual way. Four hundred dollars came in when we played music in one place. Three hundred and fifty dollars came in ... . We have never had money come in this way before."

I thought about the prosperity scriptures I had been praying back at the trailer. I had never prayed these types of scriptures before, and certainly never in this way. I would say, "Lord, all the members of my family are tithers, so we know that You have opened the windows of Heaven and have poured out blessings upon us that we can't even contain. You have rebuked the devourer for our sakes. We give, and therefore, it will be given unto us. Good measure, pressed down, shaken together and running over men will give unto our bosoms." That wasn't hard, and it hadn't taken long to say, but I felt that the money coming in to my children in Portland was a direct result of my praying those scriptures.

Other things happened while we were in Portland. It was as though I was watching a panoramic movie of events that had changed since I had been there the year before, and it seemed to me that these changes were all related to the prayers that had been going up back at the trailer. I had tapped into something awesome in prayer, something that worked and that worked quickly.

I went back home to Indiana and cared for Les until his passing in 1995, and I used this new way of prayer as a means of coping with that situation — the most difficult I had ever faced. There it was again — the force of suffering pressing me to God. When his care would begin to overwhelm me, I would remind myself, "It's time for the Scriptures." Each time, as I began praying the Scriptures, the presence of God would come into my heart. How sweet it was to abide in His presence! His presence sustained me.

I could not have realized it at the time, but I was birthing something. I was praying into existence my own future ministry, one that God was to give me after the passing of my beloved husband. This truth would lead me to write my book *Praying In Your Future*. In the book, I encouraged others to pray the wonderful plan that God has in His heart for them. I knew that they could burst forth into the stream of God's blessings and declare, "At last, it's happening to me too."

How exciting! Not only was I learning about *Unlocking the Heavens*, but I would eventually teach these secrets to others.

Chapter Five

Uniting Five Scriptural "To Do's"

Rejoice evermore. Pray without ceasing. In every thing give thanks: for this is the will of God in Christ Jesus concerning you. 1 Thessalonians 5:16-18

Scientific studies are now proving as never before that when the cells of our bodies receive proper nutrition they grow normally and take on the pattern intended for them. The DNA of the cells is strong and able to resist sickness and abnormal growth when the cells are properly nourished. This discovery holds for many people great promise of breakthrough healing from many different sicknesses.

The same is true in the spiritual sense. When Jesus becomes our Savior, He lives in us. He becomes our DNA. He is not sick, He is not deformed, and He is not weak. When we feed on the proper spiritual food, the perfect DNA pattern in us performs as it was intended, bringing our affairs into harmony with God's plan. The life of Christ living in us and ministering through us is the secret to wholeness and fruitfulness. What a spiritual breakthrough this represents! But what is the spiritual manna we require to maintain perfect spiritual health? It is surely to be found in God's Word.

In my very early days of studying prayer, I discovered five things that the Scriptures urged me to do. I knew that Jesus had left me a wonderful inheritance, and when I noticed these five instructions in the Bible, I thought they might be keys to unlock His treasures. Three of the five commands were from this passage in Paul's first letter to the Thessalonians: (1) *Pray without ceasing* (1 Thessalonians 5:17), (2) *Rejoice evermore* (1 Thessalonians 5:16), and (3) *In every thing give thanks* (1 Thessalonians 5:18). The other two were (4) *In his law doth he meditate day and night* (Psalm 1:2 and Joshua 1:8) and (5) *Abide in me, and I in you* (John 15:4).

At the beginning, I asked myself, "How can I do five different things at once?" How can I meditate on the Word of God and pray at the same time? How can I be joyful always and still pray my concerns? How can I abide in the Lord and meditate on the Scriptures at the same time? How can I give thanks in everything as part of prayer?" It was all a mystery to me, and I told the Lord I didn't think it could be done.

When I began to apply my newly learned prayer strategies, I realized that they embodied all five areas of what the Word of God instructs us to do all the time. Putting it all into one package was dynamite for me, and it would soon burst open the heavens and put my life squarely into the stream flowing with joyous blessings from the very throne of God.

How I rejoiced! I had always thought my life in Christ

should have a taste of this kind of glory, and now I was experiencing it. I was enjoying the presence of the Lord, rejoicing in it, thanking Him in it, making prayer a permanent part of my thought life, meditating on His promises day and night, and learning to abide in Him. How wonderful it was!

With some of my prayer notebooks, it would take only a few minutes to pray the prayer page for the specified day, but I learned to want to give more time to it. I meditated on the Word by savoring the message of each promise, thinking about it as I prayed. I also meditated on individual words within the prayer, and sometimes new thoughts and insights came to me from them. I contemplated each phrase and let each one speak to me. I paused often to let the words of the prayer soak into my spirit, taking time to feel and experience the impact of the words.

Most of my prayers became thanksgiving prayers, prayers of gratitude, and I tried to get my focus on the Lord and to speak to Him with my heart full of love. I even got in the habit of smiling or grinning at Him as I was doing it.

Sometimes I was overwhelmed with awe at what the Word of God said was mine. I was in awe that the Lord would die to give me the full riches of His Kingdom, and my heart melted with love for Him.

I wanted to pray with faith, and since I believed I had what I was asking for when I prayed, I began to think how I felt now that I had it. How happy I was!

I had learned that if I prayed according to the will of God, I would have what I was asking for:

And this is the confidence that we have in him, that, if we ask any thing according to his will, he heareth us: and if we know that he hear us, whatsoever we ask, we know that we have the petitions that we desired of him.   1 John 5:14-15

What better way to be sure I was praying in the will of God than to pray His Word, to meditate on His Law. I knew that it contained His will. When I prayed the Scriptures, therefore, I could feel secure that I was praying correctly. This made me bold and confident before the Lord.

There seemed to be more of a connection and joy with the presence of the Lord if I prayed these scriptures out loud, so I did that as often as I could.

Nothing at all was said in these five biblical "to do's" about focusing on the problem. I found that the more time I spent agreeing with Heaven, the more Heaven would be manifested in my earthly realm. The more time I spent praying and meditating on an earthly problem, the more that problem seemed to become locked into my situation, and I could not receive answers for it.

I had a good friend who, through the years, would call me to ask for prayer for her extended family. But despite her efforts at prayer, she never seemed to receive the answers she needed. Then she learned the prayer skills I have laid out here, and she began to put them into practice. It wasn't long before God was doing amazing miracles for her. A nephew, whom she had been praying for for many years, was saved and resurfaced to become a part of the family again. Her family had a wedding for the newly saved nephew, and it was like a Fourth of July celebration. Popping up throughout the festivities were not earthly fireworks, but powerful shafts of glory everywhere she looked.

What had changed in this woman's situation? Before, her heart had ached with compassion over the various problems she saw in her family members, and she would dwell on those problems in prayer. Now, she wonders if maybe she was actually binding them to the problems, rather than helping them. Wouldn't it be ironic if she was the one keeping them from getting their answers all along?

This new method of prayer, being seated in heavenly places in Christ Jesus, is so much more fun than the old. What a fellowship! What a joy divine! I call this my "no-sweat" praying. God was preparing me for *Unlocking the Heavens*, so that I could receive more and more from His hand.

Chapter Six

My Granddaughters Learn to Use These Strategies

Now also when I am old and grayheaded, O God, forsake me not; until I have shewed thy strength unto this generation, and thy power to every one that is to come. Psalm 71:18

In July of 1995, I took four of our granddaughters out to the RV trailer for a prayer retreat. They were between the ages of eight and twelve. Three of them were children of our son and were visiting from Nashville, Tennessee, and the other was the child of our daughter who was then living in our home.

I wanted to teach them all the things I had learned about prayer. I had them take their Bibles, and they took turns reading a scripture and then praying like they already had what the passage promised. After a while, one of the girls put her hand to her heart and said, "Oh, Grandma, it feels so good in here. Can we do this when we get home?" They all sighed in agreement. The Lord's presence had come to them as they prayed.

This caused me to remember the promise of Psalm 71:18, one of those from my early scripture notebook, and one that I had prayed many times concerning my family. I felt that the promise of this scripture was being manifested before my eyes.

I took the girls from Nashville to their home over Labor Day weekend, and we made prayer notebooks for them. Their mother had gotten out scriptures that she put on index cards years ago at Bible college, and I had my scripture prayer notebook. I took these scriptures and made a page for each day of the week.

We did a page each labeled "Mother," "Father," "Children," "Music Ministry" and "Prosperity," and we placed promises concerning each one on that particular page. This would be the forerunner of my *Miracle Grow Family Prayer Book.*

I asked the children what it was they would like God to do for them, and they all said at once, "We want a house of our own." I wondered how that could happen for them. Their mother had a job, but our son was a musician and had gone to Nashville to find work in the local music industry. So far, he hadn't found what he was looking for. How could they hope to have a home of their own anytime soon?

I said, "I know what I will do. I will put the promise of God to Abraham into each of your prayer books. It says that God will bless us in the land He has given us (see Deuteronomy 28:8). It is part of Abraham's blessings that became ours when Jesus hung on the tree (see Galatians 3:13)."

God did a great miracle for those grandchildren. By the end of the following month, their dad had the necessary down payment on a home God had reserved for them.

Another one of our families began to pray the same prayer, for they were looking for a home too. I told them I would agree with them. When I pray, I always include the entire family. Why limit a prayer to just one branch of the family?

This family took longer to find a house, so I prayed often, "Lord, our whole family is blessed in the land You have given us." Eventually, they got their house.

Some of us in the family were not even asking for a different home, but by the end of two and a half years, all five households within our family (including mine) were in new homes. Our old house had become a burden for me to maintain. I no longer had time to do things I had always enjoyed over the thirty-five years we had lived there — like raking the leaves from the nine trees in the yard. I was able to sell the home and move into a condominium that proved to be much better suited to my new life of travel for the Lord.

Molly (who had been living in our home and raising four children on her own) was able to buy a lovely split-level home in a beautiful neighborhood. What a miracle that was! She worked for a lawyer who was handling an estate auction which included a home, and no one else bid on it. Molly knew what the law would allow as a minimum bid, and that turned out to be exactly what the bank would loan her on the home. The heirs of the property were willing to let it go at that price, so Molly got her home.

Molly's daughter wanted prayer books for the members of her family also. Her mother helped me decide what promises to put in their books. It had been six years since the children's father had left the home, and since that time he had worked very hard and didn't have much time to visit the children. We put in their books the promise of Malachi 4:6, *"And he shall turn the heart of the fathers to the children."* And that is exactly what happened. Their father suddenly began to have more time for them. He even invited them to come and visit him. The boys began to work with him at times, and since then they have all developed a very loving relationship with him.

I created a booklet with my desktop publisher and called it *Miracle Grow Family Prayer Book*, using the *Family Prayer Book* as a basis. You know what happens to your flowers when you put Miracle-Gro® on them: They begin to look better than your neighbor's plants. We wanted that same "better" look for our family, and that is what was happening.

Many wonderful and heartwarming things were happening to us. It was like a constant flow from Heaven. Relationships were changing, and there was more love between the members of the family. We were *Unlocking the Heavens* through these effective prayer strategies. Could this mean that there would be no more trials? Surely not.

Chapter Seven

Bigger Battles, Bigger Victories

For all this they sinned still, and believed not for his wondrous works. Therefore their days did he consume in vanity, and their years in trouble.

Psalm 78:32-33

The Lord had said to the Israelites, "I *have* given you the land," but they had to fight for it. The land was already theirs, but they had to take it. This proved to be another of the important prayer strategies God wanted to teach me, so that I could believe more fully for the wonders He had promised me in His Word.

When a person learns that he has received an inheritance, he immediately wants to know the details. He is anxious about whom to see, what must be signed and when the things contained in the inheritance will finally be in his possession to do with as he wills. He may become very possessive about the whole matter, in an attempt to guard what is to be his from would-be interlopers. In this, too, we are very much like the Israelites.

The children of Israel did not take their land all at once. They took it a little at a time. Some of the land was easy for them to take, but other parts required them to do serious battle. And we must not be afraid of battles either. The bigger the battle, the bigger the testimony we can have when we overcome. The bigger the battle, the bigger the victory that lies ahead for us. A new battle was about to surface in our family.

We had been going along great for about two and a half years, and hardly a week had gone by without our receiving good news from one family member or another about being blessed. Then the bottom seemed to fall out from under one of our family structures.

I always tell people that when they have a trial they should pray the prayer notebooks more, and when our family crisis came, I followed my own advice. Many days I would pray for this serious family situation out of my prayer strategy notebooks, sometimes for four to six hours or more. This would put my focus on the answers more than on the problem, and I had to practice many hours before I could do this successfully. It is always easy to get caught up with the problem.

What was most important to me was to maintain a right spirit. I had to make sure that I harbored no unforgiveness. This is basic to receiving God's blessings. It wasn't a matter of who was right and who was wrong. I had to be right in my spirit. I could not afford to harbor the sin of unforgiveness or bitterness.

Was I praying for everyone to be blessed? If I wasn't, I had to change that.

Did I have peace in my heart? Many times I didn't, and

in those times, it would take much longer to pray. I first had to pray until my heart was right and I had peace. Then I knew that I was on God's answering ground.

I was sure that the more I kept my mind on Heaven's answers, the more I would see those answers manifest in this earthly situation. I also had to develop some serious weapons of warfare:

> *(For the weapons of our warfare are not carnal, but mighty through God to the pulling down of strong-holds;) casting down imaginations, and every high thing that exalteth itself against the knowledge of God, and bringing into captivity every thought to the obedience of Christ.*   2 Corinthians 10:4-5

I was in a war. The enemy was trying to build a strong-hold in my mind about the situation. I was tempted to think about it day and night. Every detail of it was like a suction cup, clinging to me and pulling me to it. I had to labor to come into a rest in prayer. I had to put a little sweat into my "no-sweat" praying.

The Bible says that we must cast down *"imaginations."* What a battle that was! I had to bring every thought into line with what the Word of God said. This was the point where I could win or lose the battle. I had to work to win, and it was definite "work."

As I learned to do these things in prayer, I began to see many good things come out of our situation. Old things began passing away, and all things began to become new. We were on our way to obtaining a testimony.

I cannot think of any problem in my life that hasn't

worked out for good. As Les would have said, "Why should God stop now?" Even in the heat of the battle, we were on our way to learning more about *Unlocking the Heavens.*

Chapter Eight

The "Go-Ye" Scriptures

And he said unto them, Go ye into all the world.
Mark 16:15

As I have said before, when I first began to make my scriptural prayer books, God would light up certain scriptures for me. Among these scriptures, there were many about going forth. At the time, I wasn't sure exactly what these verses meant for me. I wasn't interested in going forth into all the world. My only desire at that moment had been to see my son saved and the other members of my family blessed. Nevertheless, I wrote the many "Go-Ye" scriptures He gave me in the prayer book, and I would pray them, along with the other topics. There are so many of these "Go-Ye" scriptures that this is the only topic that merits two pages in my *Prayer Strategy Resource Book.*

The Scriptures tell us that we already have all we need to go forth. The enabling is already within us. It is a part of the salvation package. Among other things, we are told:

1. We are *chosen* and *ordained* to go and bring forth fruit (John 15:16).
2. We *have* received power to go into the world (Acts 1:8).
3. We *are* already Christ's ambassadors. God is pleading through us for others to be reconciled to Christ (2 Corinthians 5:20).
4. We follow Christ; He has made us to become fishers of men (Mark 1:17).
5. I have asked for this, so now I have boldness and utterance to speak, as I ought to speak (Ephesians 6:19-20).
6. I believe on Jesus, so I now can do the works He did (John 14:12).
7. I am now doing the good work that He has planned for me to do (Ephesians 2:10).
8. I have received my apostleship to make disciples among the nations (Romans 1:5-6).
9. Signs follow me, for I am a believer (Mark 16:17-20). I go forth and preach everywhere, and He confirms my words with signs following.

Over time, the meaning of these verses became more clear to me, and God gave me a ministry to share with other people. The passion of my heart these days is for the various soldiers in God's great army. Many of His soldiers, who have gone to Bible school or have studied the Word of God in other ways, have prayed and have done all they know to do, yet nothing seems to be happening for them. Consequently, the visions of their hearts have died. They have come to the conclusion that God has chosen to use only a few, and for some reason they are not among those chosen few.

This is clearly not true. God's plan is for *"whosoever will."* This means anyone who belongs to Christ can have "a piece of the action." It doesn't matter what you look like, how smart you are, whether you have talent or how bad your past was, God has a plan of action for you, and He is the Activator.

One of Les's favorite scriptures was this:

> *For if there be first a willing mind, it is accepted according to that a man hath, and not according to that he hath not.*   2 Corinthians 8:12

This verse really relates to giving, but Les understood it to mean that God expects us to work for Him with the talents we have. He does not expect us to do what we cannot do.

During the years Les was home studying with me, he would drill that scripture into me. He wanted to assure me that what I had was enough. Although I was the least in my family as I grew, although I had not achieved great success in my studies and was not especially talented, God could use me. And he was right.

This is why I'm so excited these days, why my heart is ablaze for others. If God can use me, He can use anyone. This promise of just doing with what I have has been spoken to me hundreds of times since God began sending me out.

When I made up my first prayer notebooks for the family, I printed them by hand. They didn't look all that great, but I was doing it with what I had and not with what I didn't have. Later, my pastor taught me to use the computer to make my notebooks. The spell-check didn't work all the time, and I was not a good speller, so I didn't even notice the difference. I occasionally received comments from others about misspelled words in my books, but I refused to be embarrassed by it. God only expected me to do with what I had. I would continue to improve my books and the message of them as I went.

When I eventually went to Africa, the pastor who had invited me told me there would be four services a day, and that would require four messages a day. I didn't have many messages (I had only four), but I went in faith. If God had opened the door for me to go, and He only expected me to do with what I had and not what I didn't have, then He would make a way. As it turned out, other pastors spoke twice a day. God gave me extra messages on the plane, and I came home with at least one message left over that I had never given. This promise of God gave me the courage to go when I felt inadequate and "in over my head."

I had prayed the "Go-Ye" scriptures over the years, but when I began to pray them like I already had them, like they were already mine, the life in God's promises was activated in me, and the promises began to become reality in my life. It all happened so miraculously that it seemed like I was just going along for the ride. Things were happening to me without my trying to make them happen.

I love the words of Psalm 44:3:

> *We didn't fight for this land; we didn't work for it*
> *— it was a gift! You gave it, smiling as you gave it,*
> *delighting as you gave it.*   Psalm 44:3, MES

Our part is just to believe it and say it, and God's part is to manifest it. He delights to do it, for it brings glory to Him.

I learned all these precepts late in life, and after Les passed away in 1995, God began to send me out. I was already sixty-five years old. It all seemed impossible, but God did many things to make my going both possible and fruitful:

1. He gave me a message from the simple things that had happened in my own life.
2. He opened doors for me and gave me invitations to speak that took me across this country and into Kenya and Russia.
3. He gave me the boldness to speak.
4. He gave me signs following my ministry, as people to whom I was ministering began to break forth into God's loving plan for their lives.
5. He provided the money for me to go and to have my prayer notebooks printed.
6. He made me a soul-winner. It just happened as I went. There was no striving, for He had the people who crossed my path prepared to receive.

All of this was a result of my having faithfully prayed the "Go-Ye" scriptures. It sounds very simple now, and it is, but I had to give time to praying the scriptural promises. I received what the Scriptures promised in the same way we receive salvation. I believed it with my heart, and then I confessed it with my mouth.

When I lead people in prayer to accept Jesus as their Savior, and then they say, "I don't feel anything," I don't let them believe that because they didn't feel anything, they didn't receive. I assure them they already have it by faith, and I encourage them to say it with their mouths. We can receive everything that belongs to us in the Bible this same way, and we can take the Gospel to the ends of the Earth in the same way.

We are not telling God what we want; we are praying what He wants for us. We are praying His Word and allowing Him to orchestrate every part of our lives. He has a unique plan for each of us, and He will bring it forth as we believe Him:

> *That is what is meant by the Scriptures which say that no mere man has ever seen, heard or even imagined what wonderful things God has ready for those who love the Lord.*
>
> 1 Corinthians 2:9, TLB

God has a great plan for each of us that can come forth as we begin *Unlocking the Heavens* through *Effective Prayer Strategies.*

Chapter Nine

Putting the "Go Ye" Into Action

*I know you well; you aren't strong, but you have
tried to obey and have not denied my Name. Therefore I have opened a door to you that no one can
shut.*   Revelation 3:8, TLB

I traveled to Ashland, Virginia, to hear Ruth Ward Heflin, author of the *Glory* series of books (Hagerstown, MD:
McDougal Publishing, 1990, 2000). She was preaching at
the campground her parents established there. While I was
there, I met Christopher Ndungu, a pastor from Nakuru,
Kenya. The Lord had told him that when he came to the
campmeeting, he would meet a mighty man of prayer. He
had placed an important teaching on prayer within this
man, the Lord told him, and the man would come to his
church in Nakuru, and the people would be blessed.

Early one morning, the Lord told Christopher to get
up and go walking, and he would meet the mighty man
he was looking for. Since I was the only one he saw out
walking that morning, he greeted me and kept on going.

He didn't see anyone else, and when he got back to his cabin, he asked the Lord what this meant. "I only met a poor old lady," he lamented. He had been expecting to meet someone wealthy who could help him financially with the development of his ministry.

Later that day, a friend and I sat by Christopher at lunch, and he told us of his vision. My friend spoke up and said, "Ruth has some excellent teachings on prayer." When she said that, Christopher realized that I was the person he had been looking for and invited me to Kenya for crusades.

Years ago, I had heard T.L. Osborn say, "You have dreams and visions or maybe just a particular thought of what you would like to do. Always be looking for a door to open, and when it does, go through that door. It may not be comfortable, and you may expect trouble by obeying, but if you will go through the doors that open before you, you will have a ministry." I had never forgotten his words, and now there was a door that was opening to me.

This invitation was also an answer to my own prayers. I had been asking the Lord to show me people who were desperate enough to take my prayer strategies seriously. I knew they would receive God's promises if they did. The Kenyan people were the desperate people I had been praying for. I hadn't expected to find them so far away.

Over the following months, our communications with Christopher broke down, and it looked for a while like I would not be going to Kenya. In the meantime, I went ahead and spent the money I had been reserving for the Kenya trip to pay for a trip to Russia with my pastor to do team teaching in January of 1997.

Before time for the Russian trip came, however, some

additional money came in to me, and I began to wonder if the Lord did indeed want me to go to Africa after all. Sure enough, when I got home from Russia, there was an invitation from Pastor Christopher for me to come to Kenya for an Easter crusade.

My pastor was not very happy about this invitation. He felt responsible for me since I was a widow, and he didn't know Christopher. He wondered what I was getting myself into.

I got before the Lord and prayed, "Lord, You have provided the message; You have provided the money; You have provided the open door; now I just need You to let my pastor feel good about this. If not, I can't go."

I got a letter from Christopher saying that the mayor of Nakuru was sending him to New York on business. He would be in our country for a couple of weeks. I called him and asked if he would be free to attend a meeting with some of our mission people in Toledo, Ohio, and then come to visit us in Anderson, Indiana. He agreed.

Christopher roomed with my pastor in Ohio, and they drove together to Indiana. When they arrived, my pastor said to me by phone, "Christopher is a precious brother in the Lord." The Lord had brought Christopher all the way from Africa to make my pastor feel at peace over the situation so that I could go to Kenya. The way was now clear.

Two days later, my pastor, Christopher and I were together planning the trip, and that afternoon, I went out to pay for my airline ticket. I had reserved the flights, just in case everything worked out, and the reservation was due to lapse that afternoon. God had worked just in time. He was helping me discover about *Unlocking the Heavens* for the nations of the world.

Chapter Ten

Prayer Strategies in Africa

Come over into Macedonia, and help us.
Acts 16:9

As in many churches in Kenya, Christopher's people were people of prayer. They prayed and fasted two days each week (Monday and Tuesday), they prayed all night every Friday night, and they would take turns praying around-the-clock the rest of the time. Still, they were much like me in the early years of my adventures in prayer in that they had not been receiving many answers.

When I got there, Christopher asked me what I was planning to teach on. I told him "Prayer Strategies" and "Prospering" and "Tithing."

He said, "Oh, no, Sister Ruth, you can't teach our people on tithing. You don't understand how poor they are." He went on and on for a while with this impassioned plea.

I said, "Tithing and giving are the keys to prospering, and your people will not prosper without knowing the secret of tithing." He eventually relented and permitted me to teach on tithing and its relationship to prosperity.

A year and a half later, Christopher came to America again and wrote a testimony which is printed in the back of my *Prayer Strategy Resource Book*. I had had no idea how "bad off" his church had really been when they began to use these prayer strategies. Their problems were huge. Some eighty percent of the people had been unemployed. They had no money to pay the rent on their building. There was no electricity in the church. On top of that, the people were suffering from many sicknesses and demonic oppressions.

When they got my prayer books and learned simple scriptural skills for effective prayer, doors began to open for them. Members began to be blessed, and they became more responsible to the church and started tithing. Now sixty percent of the people had work, versus twenty percent or less before.

Every Sunday, new people were coming into the church. Among the existing members, hatred and disunity disappeared, and the people began working together in unity and love more than ever before. I was grateful to God, for He had done the work.

While we were in Nakuru, my traveling companion Sue Showalter and I stayed with the mayor of the city, Alicen Chelaite. She was the first woman mayor of Nakuru, and she also happened to be a Christian. Alicen set many reforms for her city in motion, and as a result, the head of her political party had turned away from her and taken many party members with him. Party meetings were marked by infighting and disunity. Reports of this squabbling filled the local newspaper.

Sue and I had a women's meeting the final afternoon

of the crusade at Christopher's church, and we taught on "How a Woman Can Build Up Her Home." We thought the ladies needed their own prayer books, so we had a family book printed there in Nakuru for them. On the front page, we had the scriptural title "Unity." We told the ladies to pray that page each day for the mayor, so that God would break down the wall of enmity and bring peace through the cross.

The next day we went to the mayor's church and had the same type of meeting for the women. There, too, we handed out the prayer books. Two nights later, when we came back to the mayor's manse, everyone met us at the door, all talking at once. Their story was encouraging. They had held a political meeting at the manse that evening, and the opposition members had come in with smiles and laughter instead of anger. After everyone had sat down together, the rebel members now said they were ready to lay aside their differences so that they could be a unified party again.

Before we left the city, the mayor's pastor came to say good-bye. He reported that the women of his church were already giving reports of good things happening in their homes after just three days of praying these prayers.

We were now on our way to Busia near the Uganda border to do church planting. The people there also learned to pray with these skills, and now there are three churches flourishing in that area.

Later, we heard many good reports from Kenya. Emily, the mayor's house girl, memorized most of the book while we were there. She reported, during the summer of 1998, that her mother had been in the hospital in a coma with malaria and was not expected to live. Emily sat by her mother's bed and read aloud from the *Prayer Strategy Resource Book* until her mother was raised up — healed.

In Nakuru, the people continued to pray the "Unity" page for the city. Soon, ten churches were able to come together. They rented the largest stadium in Nakuru for a joint meeting. This type of united effort had never happened in that city before.

Under deep conviction, the Christians confessed their sins and the sins of their people. Then they wrote those sins on old rags, put the rags in a dumpster and burned them. The Spirit of the Lord came down, and many sinners were saved and many sick people were healed that day. It was awesome what God was doing.

How wonderfully rewarding it was to have been able to help many others understand the secrets of *Unlocking the Heavens* and to see the fruit of their *Effective Prayer Strategies.*

When I saw what power was loosed when a group of people agreed in prayer, I also knew in my heart that if any group of people in a given city would sit in the heavenlies with Christ, thanking Him and giving Him glory, while bathing the city with the victory scriptural prayers from my book *Praying For Your City*, that city could easily have a revival.

Chapter Eleven

Blessing and Not Cursing

But I say unto you, Love your enemies, bless them that curse you, do good to them that hate you, and pray for them which despitefully use you, and persecute you. Matthew 5:44

As I was growing up, my family thought if they could tell me what was wrong with me, I would get the message, shape up and be better. No doubt they had cause to think I needed this help. My mother noted that I was a "scamp," and laughingly said I had too much "shanty Irish" in me. (For those who are unfamiliar with these phrases, she was saying that I was mischievous.)

I did not thrive under that treatment, however, even though it sounds right and practical, and I am sure they meant well by it. The outcome was that I was sickly and did not do well in school. As I have said, I spent five months of my senior year sick in bed. After the thyroid operation, I had a little more energy. I was able to do well in school and finished the twelfth grade the next year by going to high school in the morning and then to the university in the afternoon.

That year something else happened that helped me more than anything else. I started dating Les. Five days before our first date, I experienced my last sickness and then came into health. I believe new health came to me because Les loved me unconditionally. He never seemed to notice any of my faults — of which I am sure there were many. After we were married, I felt strengthened to be a better person, and I believe this too was due to being in this loving environment. Les knew how to build up his home rather than tear it down.

For example, after Les retired and came home to pray with me, the wife of an elder came to our house one day. She was thinking about getting a divorce from her husband, and proceeded to tell us her reasons. She finally paused, and Les said, "Bless, and curse not."

She wanted to know what Les meant by that. When he repeated what he had said, she still didn't understand. He showed her the scripture I began the chapter with. It is part of the Sermon on the Mount. Les had, of course, quoted from Romans:

> *Bless them which persecute you: bless, and curse not.*
> Romans 12:14

Finally, the lady's face lit up with a big smile. "Oh, I get it," she said. Then she picked up her purse and left.

We talked to that lady several months later, and she told us that what Les said that day had changed her life.

As she left our house that very day, she had begun to bless her husband instead of thinking and saying negative things about him. As a result, their marriage turned around, and she was now very happy with her husband.

As we have seen, an effective strategy for prayer is letting go of the problem. When we pray and think about the problem, we bind that problem to the person, and he or she can never be set free from the darkness the problem has put on his or her life. When we pray or meditate on the answer, instead of on the problem, we gain the higher vision, the blessing God has prepared for us, and that looses the person from the powers of darkness. This leads us also to conclude that we must bless and not curse.

One of the most powerful pages in my *Prayer Strategy Resource Book* is entitled "Forgiving and Blessing." I think perhaps one of the biggest problems Christians have today is not being free to forgive. They will say, "Lord, forgive me for my feelings toward (<u>The Person's Name</u>)," but then they go away not feeling any different. The problem is still there to plague their souls. Nothing has changed.

Many women, in particular, are very sensitive in this regard. They feel things deeply. They sometimes want to warn a loved one, and if that loved one doesn't listen, those women walk away in hurt and pain. "This is not right," they say, and of course, they are right. But their reaction to the slight has created a much larger problem than existed before. This is the way dark hurts and bitterness take root in many hearts.

I had my own problem in this regard. Someone whom I loved very deeply hurt me, and I felt the pain of it day and night. I didn't want to feel pain. I wanted to forgive. I knew that not forgiving this person was sin, and I confessed this sin many times. Still, I was somehow not free from my feelings. I still had them.

I had often said that these prayer strategies will work for any problem, so I made the page entitled "Forgiving and Blessing," filled it with promises from the Word of God related to this subject, and began to pray them. I also had told people that if they had a big problem, they should pray these scriptural prayers often. I prayed that page three times a day, and before long, I began to be loosed from the torment I was experiencing.

At certain intervals over the following months and years, the problem would try to come back. When this happened, I put in some extra time praying the promises of that powerful page, and God would give me the victory.

While I was putting those forgiveness scriptures together, I couldn't help but notice that praying a blessing on those who have hurt us was woven into the fabric of many of the scriptural admonitions. Could praying a blessing on people be an antidote to the problem of unforgiveness? I decided to try it.

I would bless the person often. I would say, "I bless (The Person's Name) with Heaven's blessings and earthly joys," "I lift (him/her) up into your arms of love, Lord," or "Your glory is on (him/her), Lord." I found that the person who was involved in my problem would indeed be blessed in many ways. Other people noticed it too and commented on it. Most importantly, I was set free to love.

Ed Silvoso, who wrote the book *That None Should Perish*, created a ministry called Lighthouses of Prayer in

Argentina. A great revival broke out there in a large metropolitan area of that country when many Christian people began praying for their neighbors. They had been asked by their leaders not to pray about the bad things they knew about a certain neighbor, but to concentrate on blessing that person and bringing him or her peace. The powers of darkness were broken by this simple way of praying, and revival was released over that city.

This same thing will happen for every one of us, for our homes, for our communities and for our nations as we learn the secret of blessing and not cursing. This is an important key to *Unlocking the Heavens*.

Chapter Twelve

Content With Being Abased

I know both how to be abased, and I know how to abound: every where and in all things I am instructed both to be full and to be hungry, both to abound and to suffer need. I can do all things through Christ which strengtheneth me.   Philippians 4:12-13

In the 1970s, Les and I went to a meeting together. When the speaker had finished his message, he invited couples to come to the front so that he could pray for them. Les and I went forward.

When he prayed for us, the man said the Lord showed him that we had money problems. This surprised us, because our business was doing very well and we had no children in college at the time. It was actually one of our better times financially, we told him. When we said that, the speaker looked puzzled. "Watch your money," he said, "for you are going to have problems."

Those words didn't seem to bother my husband, but they did upset me. We women always want to know that we are financially secure. If crisis was coming, I wanted to be ready. I prepared for it by finding scriptures on the Lord taking care of His people in famine. I particularly loved the words of the psalmist who said he had never seen the righteous forsaken or his seed begging bread. I put all the promises I could find in this regard in my little scripture notebook, and I began to pray them along with the rest of my scriptures.

When Les decided to retire and come home to pray and study the Word with me in 1980, I thought this might be the time the man had spoken of. This would surely be our time of financial crisis.

Les faced this trial with great assurance. He loved books about the great men of faith like George Müller, Hudson Taylor and Smith Wigglesworth and could not forget the fact that they had never asked anyone for help. These men of faith had determined to trust only the Lord, and Les vowed that, whatever happened, we would do the same.

The money from the sale of the dental lab kept us for about a year and a half, but then it ran out, and with nothing coming in, things quickly became very tight for us. The next time our car license came up for renewal, we didn't have enough to renew it, and the car sat for a year without a license.

There were benefits, however. We had a wonderful year in Bible study together — the best ever, and we enjoyed walking more than usual. Although we didn't mention our dilemma to anyone, people from the church offered to come by and take us to services, and we enjoyed their fellowship. It was also the time when Les's eyesight was failing, and it was a relief for me that he wasn't driving.

Never once in that year did either of us ever say, "I wish we had the car on the road." We were doing just fine without it. We were content.

We had made a decision to eat healthy foods. If we were not going to have much money, I wanted to spend what we did have on foods that would be good for us. We stopped buying white flour and sugar and joined a natural food co-op where we could buy sunflower seeds and other things we enjoyed very cheaply. I was able to buy wheat directly from a grain elevator for three dollars a bushel. It was out of season at the time, and they were out of grain, but they said they would find a bushel for me. I believe they swept it up off the floor of the bin, for the bushel they sold us was very dirty.

I washed the wheat, drained off the dirty water and picked out the chaff. Then I laid the grain out on cookie sheets to dry. While I was busy talking on the phone, I would look through the wheat for anything else that didn't seem to belong in it. After the wheat was clean and dry, I used a coffee grinder to grind it. When my oven went out, I made stovetop biscuits out of that whole wheat.

We always had something to eat during that time. Many times the Lord would show me what I had in the house and how I could make a meal of it. I used food that had been in my cupboard for years, until finally even the cupboard became bare.

That Christmas after we first ran out of money, our son, who was in Bible college at the time, let us know that he was bringing a girl from school home for the holidays. The refrigerator was pretty bare, and although Les and I always had enough for a few meals ahead for ourselves, the thought of feeding a stranger seemed like a great feat. I talked to the Lord about it and told Him that I didn't want to be ashamed.

Several days later, some friends came to visit us. We hadn't seen them in a while. We had attended the same church some years before. We had a nice visit, and just as they were ready to leave, they finally mentioned what they had actually come for. One of the man's ribs had separated from the muscle. It was badly swollen, and he was in great pain. There was nothing the doctor could do for him, and he wanted us to pray for him.

Les got up, went around the back of the other man's chair, put his hand very gently on the area of that rib, and prayed. When he did that, the swelling went down under his hand, the pain left, and the man was healed.

Before they left that day, the man went out to his car and brought in a sack full of frozen meat. They had just butchered, and this meat was left over from the previous year. They hoped we could make use of it. We were like a couple of children. We could hardly wait until they left to see just what was in the sack.

There were roasts, steaks and hamburger. That Christmas season, three turkeys came in, and the refrigerator was full. It was very cold outside, so we used the car (which had no plates on it) as a freezer. When our son and his friend came, we were able to feed them all our favorite dishes.

There was heavy snow and ice for six weeks straight that winter, but it didn't trouble us. We had no need to go to the store. There was plenty of food in the house.

Whether there was food or not, we often fasted in the

mornings. We would pray and study the Bible until mid-afternoon, and then I would make us each a big bowl of cereal, using my ground wheat. I mixed it with sunflower seeds and nuts, and sometimes even applesauce or frozen bananas. Yum! That felt so good to our hungry stomachs. It was more like a dessert.

There was an apple tree in our churchyard that had never produced anything but knurly, wormy apples. Just when we needed its fruit, however, it began to produce large, lovely, good-tasting apples. When we went to church for prayer, I would pick up the apples that had fallen to the ground. I pared them while we prayed, and then I made applesauce and apple butter from them when I got home. That apple butter was awfully good on my stovetop biscuits.

There were black walnut trees in our neighborhood, and they were producing big crops in those days. Les and I enjoyed them.

I read that the Indians had eaten acorns and how they prepared them, so I gathered acorns from our yard and shelled them. I then covered them with water, brought them to a boil, poured off the water and repeated this several more times to get out all the tannic acid. When the acorns were ready to eat, they tasted like a cooked cereal, and they were very filling.

I read a book about the early New York ministry days of Pat and Dede Robertson. They would put a pot of soybeans on in the morning to cook, and someone would go to the city market and buy marked-down vegetables to add to the beans when they got home. With very little expenditure, they had a very nutritious meal. I tried Dede's soybean recipes. We liked them so much that I kept cooked soybeans in the freezer, ready to be put into many of the dishes I would make.

I approached it all as a very challenging game to be played out. We were content in our time of abasement. During that period, I was more thankful for the food I had to eat than I ever had been before. My heart was running over with gratitude. I would commonly say, "Oh, Les, just look at this plate. Look at the different kinds of food! How colorful they all are!"

One Sunday evening, we came home from church to find that someone had left a freezer for us, and the next morning we found that our refrigerator had quit working. It was the middle of the summer, so I told Les to plug in the freezer, and we put our frozen food into it. We then froze milk jugs full of water and put them in coolers to keep the other food from going bad. We didn't have money to get the refrigerator fixed for a while, so we lived that way for the next five months.

Several days after the freezer arrived, I noticed that my screen door was ajar. When I went to see why, I found three large sacks of frozen food sitting in the doorway. I had never had a freezer before, but now the Lord kept it stocked with a good supply of frozen food.

When some of the local people butchered, they had no use for some of the animal parts, especially the heart, liver and tongue, so they gave them to us. They were treats for us, and I knew how to fix them well.

We had company over a couple of times a week. We wanted to share our blessings, and Les felt we should invite those whom we didn't know very well, especially those who might not be able to invite us to their houses.

Since we didn't know these people well, conversation was sometimes strained. Les would suggest that each person bring a song, a scripture or a testimony to share, and we would take turns sharing in this way. It was a wonderfully unique experience, and the blessing of the Lord would come upon us, knitting our hearts together with joy.

It was during this time that Les, who had been a tither for many years, saw in Paul's second letter to the Corinthians a challenge to give to the poor and to missions:

> *As it is written, He hath dispersed abroad; he hath given to the poor: his righteousness remaineth for ever.*   2 Corinthians 9:9

Based on this verse, Les decided that we should give an extra tithe to the poor. He also came to believe that to "disperse (spread) abroad" meant to give to missions, so he began to set aside another tithe for missionary work. His ideas on giving seemed like a stretch to me, but he loved every minute of it. Giving was his joy.

And God was faithful to His promises. Each time we were stretched only proved to us that God was on the side of the giver. We never did without.

Early one spring day, I began to feel that I needed clothes for the warmer weather to come. At about five that morning I was praying about this. At ten that same morning, a car drove up and a lady got out carrying several garbage bags full of clothes. In those bags, she had just the clothes I had been asking God for only a few hours earlier.

When Les needed a new pair of shoes, we prayed about them. In my mind's eye, I could see a pair of new shoes in a box on a table. Not long after that, we were walking to the grocery store one day, when we passed a rummage sale in a garage. I walked into that garage, and there on a table in the back was a box with a new pair of English Walkers in it. They were being sold for three dollars. We bought them. Those shoes wore so well and so long that after Les passed away, our grandson continued to wear them for dress. He thinks they are "cool."

Only once were we severely tested with a utility bill. One cold winter, the gas company sent us a notice threatening to turn off our gas because we were late with our payment. I looked out the window often that day, but no one ever came to turn off the gas. I wondered if someone in the company office was aware of the fact that we had given money in past winters so that those who couldn't pay their gas bills would not face disconnection. Whether men knew it or not, God did, and He kept the gas man from coming that day to cut off our supply.

A day or so later, a man came to our house to visit. He had been laid off from his work. The company had given him severance pay, but he was wondering how he would survive the winter. Les asked him if he tithed. He said he couldn't afford to, but Les told him he needed to do it so that he could be blessed.

Les took a dollar out of his pocket, gave it to the man and told him it was for him to give away. Then he decided to give the man everything he had in his pockets, which was another dollar and some change. He said to the man, "I will receive a hundredfold more than I have given you, and you must learn to do the same."

That Wednesday evening, when our pastor finished his message, he said, "While I was preaching, the Lord told me to take up an offering for a family in the church. I don't want to say who it is. Just ask the Lord how much you should give and bring it up and put it in the basket." He gave the offering to us that night, and it was a hundred times what Les had given the man. That went a long way toward getting our bills paid. We were "over the hump" and would never go through that same kind of trial again.

After our car sat through all that year without a license, it was getting rusty. I talked to the Lord about this, because I was sure He didn't want us to be ashamed. As Les prayed, he could see in his mind a gray car, although he didn't know what kind of car it was. Then, as we prayed, I began to get a picture each morning of a light gray minivan turning into our driveway.

One day, enough money came in for us to think about buying another car, and we went to a dealer to look at the vehicles he had on his lot. A red car appealed to us, and we temporarily forgot about the light gray minivan the Lord had been showing us. It was late in the day and the car dealership was about to close, so we told the man we would think about it and come back the next day.

One thing we had confirmed that day: Buying a car was going to take more money than we had anticipated. We decided that if we didn't pay our usual triple tithe on the money that had come in, we could swing the deal. We would pay our tithe to the church, but we would not give our customary tenths to the poor and to missions this time.

The next morning I asked Les if the Lord had spoken to him, and he said He had. "Was it about the tithe?" I asked, and he said it was.

I wasn't surprised, but I was disappointed. What kind of car could we get with the money we would have left? Then, the Lord spoke to my heart, "And I don't want you to be asking anyone about a car." It seemed that we would not be buying a car right away as we had been planning.

Three months went by, and one day I was visiting my daughter in Huntington, Indiana. On the way back to her house from shopping with one of her sons, we passed a large automobile dealership. It was raining hard as we went by, but for some reason I decided to pull into the lot, drive through and look at the available cars.

As I was turning around, a salesman ran out in the driving rain, tapped on the car window and asked if I was interested in a car. I told him I was interested but didn't think I had enough money to buy one. He asked me how much I had. When I told him, he agreed that I didn't have enough.

He paused to think for a moment, and then he remembered a vehicle that had come in on a trade the day before. They were still in the process of checking it out, but it might be just what I was looking for. He suggested that I park and come inside, and he would have someone bring the vehicle into the garage for me to see.

I stood by the door waiting for a few minutes. Then the door went up, and in came a light gray minivan, just like the one I had seen many times as I was praying. It took my breath away, and I whispered, "Lord, do You mean that we have enough money to get that?" It was true. The Lord enabled us to buy that lovely vehicle.

Over the years, the Lord showed us that He was concerned about the smallest need we had. One day we needed some rubber bands, and we found them along the curb when we took our walk. Apparently, the mailman had discarded them along his route.

At one point, I had a pair of hose that lasted me for two and a half years. At the end of that time, they suddenly fell apart. Just then, I was blessed with a good supply of hose.

During those years, we seldom had to labor in prayer for our needs. The promise of our supply had been recorded in my prayer book and it was all pre-prayed. His promise is:

> *He cares for them when times are hard; even in famine, they will have enough.*
>
> Psalm 37:19, TLB

Our souls were enriched during our years of abasement, and God miraculously supplied our every need. We were learning more and more about *Unlocking the Heavens*.

Chapter Thirteen

Abounding, Prospering

I know both how to be abased, and I know how to abound: every where and in all things I am instructed both to be full and to be hungry, both to abound and to suffer need. I can do all things through Christ which strengtheneth me.   Philippians 4:12-13

There is another side of the coin. Paul learned both how to be abased and how to abound, and how to be content in both cases. This is something that we all must learn. Just as Les and I had had wonderful experiences in learning to be abased and learning contentment in God's wonderful care, I found that my new strategies for prayer opened the doors to prosperity, and prospering was definitely better.

Some people still wonder if it is God's will for His people to prosper. They actually think it is bad manners to ask God to supply what they need. I understand where they are coming from. Many of us were trained in childhood that when we went to someone else's house, it would be rude to ask for a cookie, for example. Asking in that setting is considered selfish and willful. But what does God say about asking Him for what we need and want?

In Old Testament times, God told the Israelites, "I have given you the land." They didn't have anything yet, but God spoke as if it was already theirs. The Psalms declare that because the Israelites did not believe God for His wondrous works, He turned them over to vanity and trouble. Apparently there is a chastisement that goes along with not being willing to receive what God says is already ours. Not only is He willing for us to ask, but He considers it to be rude if we don't. He longs to see us prosper, and He delights in our petitions.

Our habit of tithing began in an unusual way. The church we attended in the 1950s never mentioned tithing. Still, Les saw it in the Bible and got it into his head that he wanted to tithe. When he mentioned it to me, my reply was, "Surely God doesn't expect us to tithe. We don't have anything except three little children. Tithing is for people who have the money to do it." But I could see that Les wasn't listening to what I was saying. I felt like I was going to faint, for I knew he was going to do what was on his heart, and I was sure we couldn't afford it.

That next Sunday, Les lined up the kids and me. He put five dollars in an envelope for the general fund, kept a dollar out for Sunday school, and was trying to think how to divide up ten cents among the three children. He wanted to do the right thing. God honored Les's faith and began to bless us.

The day we began tithing I was wearing a wraparound cotton dress my mother had sent me for my birthday. I had worn it every Sunday for quite a while, because it was the best dress I owned at the time. Soon, however, a box came with some beautiful clothes in it for me, and similar boxes continued to come twice a year for many years to come. I now had more clothes than I could wear. God had given to us, pressed down and running over, just as the Scriptures had said would happen if we tithed.

It wasn't long before we were tested. If we paid our tithes, it seemed that we would not have enough money for groceries one week. Les put the tithe in the offering anyway, and during the week we received a letter with just enough money in it for our needs. What a surprise for us in our new venture!

It was in 1981 that Les began to tithe to the poor and to missions. He also gave a tithe in gifts, and he put another ten percent of our income into savings. Before the year was over, however, Les had learned about a need someone had, and he gave them the money he had been saving.

That troubled me some. As the children were growing up, I sometimes said to Les, "We need to save for the children's college." His reply was that if the Lord wanted them to go to college, He could provide for it.

When the time came for the children to start college, Les's attitude hadn't changed. Since he never liked to owe money to anyone, he said that we would go as far as we could, we would pay each school bill as it came in, and if the day came that the Lord didn't supply the money and we couldn't pay, the kids could come home. Each year the Lord would supply our children's college expenses in different ways. At one point, we had three in college at the same time. We came through that period without owing anyone, although we were tested along the way.

I remember one occasion when we needed $1,000 to pay one of those college bills. We had been looking for the money to come in, but by the day it was due, nothing had shown up. Les called from the lab that day and asked me, "Has the mail come yet?" I told him it had but that there was no money in the mail.

That evening, Les went to a meeting. When he got home, he lifted the mailbox lid and looked in, just in case, and there was a letter that I was sure had not been there earlier. How it got there I never knew. In the letter was a check for $1,000. God had placed it on the heart of someone to send it. It had been meant for another need, but that particular need had already been supplied, and God knew that we needed funds for our children's college.

Once, when we desperately needed $500, an elderly man, who had never been in an accident before, came out of an alley and ran into the side of our car. The insurance check to cover the damage arrived just in time to send the college payment. We went around with a bashed-in car door for a while as we waited for money to come in to have it fixed, but we didn't mind.

We were attending a church at the time where a number of very fancy cars would be in the parking lot each week. When we parked our car, Les and I both had to get out on the driver's side because it was the other door that was smashed in. It was a little embarrassing, but the Lord didn't seem to mind that we were embarrassed, so we didn't either.

One day the Lord prompted me to give away everything that I was not using. I had always loved to save things, thinking that I would use them eventually, and they often came in very handy. Now, I cleaned out the attic, and a friend who also loved to give to others came over and loaded up her car several times with my extra things. No sooner had we done this than the Lord supplied a substantial sum of money we had been needing. Proverbs declares that I can give away and become richer in the process (see Proverbs 11:24).

Our God delights in providing for our personal needs and the needs of our ministries. Using the prayer strategies I learned enabled me to travel all over the world, paying my own way. My, I like that!

I was blessed when I heard from Africa that the people were now able to pray in their prosperity. Before, they had little or nothing, and some families were actually starving. Their sudden prosperity was a sign and a wonder to many who witnessed it. I could not provide what those people needed for food and other daily needs, but I was able to point them to the One who could. His name is Jesus.

I was thrilled when God enabled me to send money for both the land and the building for a church to be raised up in Kenya. I was blessed to have money to buy a computer to help me create prayer books, and money to have them printed. Someone asked me one day, "What mission board supports you?"

I said, "The Lord is my mission board." Who else would have provided for an "unknown" like me in the ministry? I say that to encourage others who have dreams in their hearts. God is able to supply for you too.

I heard someone say, "You know that God is sending you, when you have both an invitation and the money to go." It's true.

When Les was near death, I wondered how I would bury him. Then money came in which enabled me to purchase a burial trust package for the two of us. Six months after he passed away, I had money to buy a new car and pay cash for it. God was getting ready to send me out into the vineyard, and somehow I sensed that it was a new day.

We have had a number of testimonies come in of people prospering from praying the "Prosper" page of my *Prayer Strategy Resource Book*. God's promises are real, and we can stand on them.

Dale Carnegie once said that seventy percent of all our worries have to do with finances. If we can only trust God for our physical needs, then a large part of our worries will disappear. We can trust Him, for He has promised to supply all our needs.

Does God really care about the concerns and needs of His people? Absolutely! Will I always have enough to go out and minister? I believe if God wants me to go, He will provide. Otherwise, I will be happy to stay home and pray. I plan to be contented in whatever state I find myself. I am determined not to be demanding, but to flow in God's plan — whatever it happens to be. This proved to be another key to *Unlocking the Heavens*.

Chapter Fourteen

The Highest Realm of Prayer

You have made known to me the path of life; you will fill me with joy in your presence, with eternal pleasures at your right hand. Psalm 16:11, NIV

Many early Church fathers considered that the highest realm of prayer was simply being in the presence of God. They had very little to say about specific petitions, for they knew that many of God's purposes and plans for people's lives come forth when they get their focus on the Lord and maintain close communion with Him.

In 1980, as I have said, I was going through a physical trial and had been in bed for about three weeks. One morning, my condition worsened so that I thought I was actually going to die. I have to admit that I was frightened in that moment. To keep myself from thinking about the seriousness of my condition, I asked Les to bring some hymnbooks to my bed and was encouraged to sing to the Lord.

As I kept my focus on the Lord, as if His face was right

there before me, I was fine. If I would ease off a bit, however, the fears would come right back. When they did, I would immediately put my focus back on the Lord and on the hymns I was singing, and I was okay again. This went on for four or five hours, and during this time, I could not feel the presence of the Lord or His joy. Then, suddenly, the Spirit of God swept into the house. Les ran into the bedroom shouting, leaping for joy and praising God.

Just as suddenly, in the Spirit, it seemed that I could see into Heaven. There was a lot of light and a lot of activity, and I sensed that the activity meant that Heaven was busy fulfilling the desires of my heart. I said to myself, "Of all the books I have read on prayer, I have never read about this higher realm of prayer." I had touched something new and wonderful.

My healing started to come that day, and the Lord let me know that He would like for me to pray with focus all the time, just as I had done that day. For some reason, however, I was not able to do it.

Later, I realized that what I had experienced that day was a foretaste of things to come. As time passed, I was to meet a series of great men and women of God who had pressed into a greater place in prayer, and I was to find that what I had learned was comparable to their revelation.

In 1996, for example, after I read Ruth Ward Heflin's book *Glory*, I called her campground in Ashland, Virginia, to order some more books and was told that she would be there speaking over the Fourth of July holiday. On the spur of the moment, a friend and I decided to go hear her.

Ruth had gone to Jerusalem to serve the Lord many years before, and while she was there, the Lord had taught her many things about effective prayer. He told her that it was not as important to ask for particular things as it was to praise Him. Then He taught her to move from praise to worship and, from worship into the realm of His glory. Once in the glory, she was to stay there and commune with God, receiving revelation and strength from His very throne.

Sometimes the Lord made Ruth and her people aware of great things that had been accomplished by dwelling in the glory, and He let them know that much more could be accomplished by putting their focus on His glory than through ordinary prayer.

After Ruth had mastered this strategy, she began teaching it to others around the world, and many benefited from it. As I traveled to the campground, I was expecting to experience this "glory" for myself.

Although I put my whole heart into my search for God's glory during the days I was at the Ashland campground, nothing seemed to happen. I was very disappointed. The last night I was there, I went to bed and began to pray my scriptures and come into the Lord's presence as I had learned to do over the years. Before long, the Lord's presence came into my heart ever so sweetly, and He made me know that the glory Ruth Heflin had come to experience was the same as His joyous presence I had been experiencing through my prayer strategies. She had been receiving awesome answers to prayer, and I also had been having remarkable results. The Lord had brought me into a whole new ministry — just by praying with these new skills.

I was so deeply touched by a prophecy I read in Frances Roberts' book *Come Away, My Beloved* that I included it in the front of my *Prayer Strategy Resource Book* on a page entitled "The Dynamic of Praise." Although the prophecy does not discount prayers of petition, it shows that we can help more people in less time through becoming free in our praises. We must not analyze or try to diagnose everything, but just hold the Lord close and not let Him go. This type of prayer centers around a strong focus on the Lord.

In his book *The Final Quest* (New Kensington, PA: Whitaker House, 1996), Rick Joyner described seeing people going through various trials and struggling to get up the mountain to God and peace. He saw that some perished on the way. He himself pressed on and came to a high place where the darts of the enemy could not reach. There, he found rest and perfect peace. Later, he went back down the mountain and started rescuing others who had fallen. I found his experience to be very similar to my own.

In March of 2000, I attended a conference in Nashville, Tennessee, where Mahesh and Bonnie Chavda were speaking. They were sharing how they had come into a place in the Lord where all was peaceful and nothing was troubling their spirits. They told those of us who attended the meeting how to come into this higher realm with God and assured us that we could do it for ourselves and that we could later maintain this status after we left the conference.

They had three suggestions for us:

1. To get quiet, and fill our minds with loving God (again, the focus on Him)

2. To do this often
3. To rid our minds of other thoughts

People around me at the conference were manifesting the presence of God in many different ways. Some were slain in the Spirit, and others had holy laughter. Still, nothing seemed to be happening to me.

Mahesh and Bonnie laid hands on us all for an impartation of the anointing to be able to do what they were telling us. When I arrived home and had time to think about it, I realized: *I already know how to come into the presence of the Lord, because of my prayer strategies. I will just do this more often.* After that, it seemed that I was enabled to come into the presence of the Lord with great ease, with joy, and even with laughter.

We had come home on Monday, and by Thursday evening I had broken into this new realm. It was as if I had stepped up higher, and all was light. There was a peace I had never experienced before. There was nothing in my spirit that was static, troublesome or of concern. I felt the perfect peace *"that passes understanding."*

I was not able to stay indefinitely in this realm, but every time I was able to put effort into it, I found the experience to be absolutely delicious. There was so much joy in my heart that it seemed like I had turned a corner in my spiritual walk. There was beauty everywhere I looked.

Whenever a negative or depressive thought tried to come into my mind, I switched my thoughts and began loving Jesus. It became easier to refuse anything negative. What a relief! Everywhere I go now, I see people through

God's creative eyes, with their beautiful gifts and callings. They are like treasures unfolding before me, and I am awed.

When I got home from the Chavda meeting, I picked up a book from my shelf that I had not read for many years. It was *This Wondrous Way of Life* by an Englishman named Brother Mandus (London: L.N. Fowler & Co., Ltd., 1956). When I opened the book and began to read, I found that it was about all that I had been experiencing. Brother Mandus said:

> Whenever a problem arose, it was solved, not by fighting and straining against it, but by entering the silence, loving the Father until His peace enveloped me. In His peace, the problem was solved. It just worked its way right through so perfectly. I began to understand love, simplicity and oneness with God. (page 105)

In August of 1999, I attended a Christian Family retreat in Michigan. During the week, we were asked to write a letter to God, and then write down what we thought God was saying to us in return. We handed the letters in, and they were to be mailed to us at a later date. My letter came back to me in March before I went to the Chavda conference. What the letter had predicted that God would be doing in my life would now be coming forth in a greater measure. It said:

> I will call you higher into My presence and My will. You will be forced to live in My presence. I will or-

chestrate and train you into walking in My glory,
and My glory shall fall on others wherever you go.

And it began to happen. Sometimes, when I went somewhere for the Lord, His presence was felt in every situation, and at other times, only in vignettes here and there. I soon got the feeling, as the King's daughter, that it was just because I was there. I could sense how pleased the Lord was with me. This happened more and more as I spent quality time in His presence.

Les and I had been blessed earlier by the Rodney Howard-Browne phenomenon. In 1994, we had wintered in Lakeland, Florida. It was the winter after the revival had broken out in Carpenter's Home Church with Rodney, and he came back that year for three weeks. Les and I attended all those meetings.

We would go to the 10:00 A.M. meeting, get back home between one and two in the afternoon, eat, take a nap and be ready for the evening service. We would have to get there by 6:30 each evening to get a seat, and we would usually get home sometime between 12:00 midnight and 2:00 in the morning. What God was doing was very exciting, and we never felt sleepy during the meetings.

An Episcopal priest was attending the meetings too. He had been called to the ministry while in college and had been very reluctant to accept, but God was using him. He had raised up a small church in Lakeland and had been pastoring it for the past ten years.

The priest asked Rodney Howard-Browne why more wasn't happening with him. The answer was that he needed to soak in the presence of the Lord more. The priest did that, and God raised him up and placed him into a new ministry that was very suited to him. He left his pastorate and began to answer calls from Episcopal churches all over the country where people were hungry for revival. Everywhere he went, revival followed. I had tapped into something similar.

Some years ago, I heard Rick Joyner speak at a leaders' retreat. He told the gathering that God had showed him people going through pressings so great that they had come to their limit and felt "undone." Even though they had tried to be righteous for the Lord, they were *"as filthy rags."* The only thing left for them to do was to cling to God. If they would do this, God would break through suddenly and bring them forth into their ministries. It would be God's anointing working through them.

This, he said, would happen to some of those gathered in that very room, and it would begin about 1993. When he said this, the thought came to me that I would be one of them. Still, I had no idea of how or of what kind of ministry I would receive.

After our lunch break, I seated Les (who was afflicted by that time) in the meeting room, and I was on my way back up the aisle to do an errand when I saw Rick Joyner. He was seated at the back of the room (as was his custom, so that God could give him insights about the people), and he was beaming at me. I was surprised, for I had not spoken personally with him before. That seemed to confirm to me the message I had received that I was one of those whom God would bring forth. This thought gave me great hope over the years.

The pressings came because of Les's health. I was his

caregiver, and it was an extremely heavy responsibility. Fortunately, I had a survival technique. It was praying the scripture books with my focus on appreciating God. This brought me continually into His presence. This time of preparation was important, for it was just after Les passed away that my ministry suddenly broke through.

God is raising up a great army, and He wants to bring us forth. Many Christians have signed up for every course that is coming along because they have it in their hearts to serve God in a meaningful way. Many have lost hope that it would ever happen, but it is not a time for despair. This is God's hour to raise up all those who will give themselves over to His presence, who will learn the highest realm of prayer.

I urge you not to despise the trials that come to you, but count them as God's training ground. Rather than allow your trials to drag you down, let them bring you closer to the Lord. This is an important key to *Unlocking the Heavens.*

Chapter Fifteen

Praying In Your Future

"For I know the plans I have for you," declares the
LORD, *"plans to prosper you and not to harm you,*
plans to give you hope and a future."
Jeremiah 29:11, NIV

My heart goes out to Christians everywhere for their families. I meet many wonderful Christians who love and serve the Lord with great faithfulness, but whose hearts are crying out because of the pain they experience within their own families. I know that these prayer strategies can help people like these to resolve every difficulty of their lives, and that is why I have such a passion to spread this good news.

Over the years, I have been told by some that they considered it to be wrong to pray for your own family. "That's selfish," they'd say, "you should be praying for the lost." But the family is the basic structure of society that God has placed on Earth. The Bible is the story of families. If I don't pray for my family, who will?

My reply to people who say such things is that I pray for what God tells me to pray for. I am accountable to Him. Many years ago, I felt His calling to be a keeper at home and to raise up my family. The fact that I had many shortcomings and that things did not go as I had planned drew me away from the thought that I had all the answers and made me an intercessor, seeking God's way. I do pray for many other concerns, but I must never be guilty of failing to pray for my family. That is my first responsibility.

Wherever I have seen people begin praying with the specific prayer skills I have mentioned here, I have seen them start flowing in the stream of God's love, and I have watched them bring forth His plan for their lives and the lives of their family members as well. What joy this brings! What relief, when men and women see God's hand move for them! Of all the testimonies I receive, I rejoice most in those that relate to families. Many of them are similar to this e-mail I received recently:

> *Praise the Lord!*
> *I have been praying the* **Miracle Grow Family Prayer Book** *ever since you spoke at our Wisconsin CFO retreat. God is answering many of our prayers and family needs. Angel is doing very well with her class and passed all her tests and will graduate May 13.* [At the retreat, they had been very stressed, thinking that Angel might not pass her tests for her senior year of nursing school because she was also working full time.]
> *God has even arranged for Angel and me to go on a*

*week-long vacation — all expenses paid — to Trini-
dad and Tobago in June. Actually, Angel got to
choose where she wanted to go.*

*Plus He is healing relationships with my two sons
and their families. I want the extra copies of the
prayer books to give to them so they can pray and to
give to other families at church.*

*My job situation has improved one hundred percent.
My boss even called me into the office last week to
thank me for the good job I was doing. Praise the
Lord.*

> *Lots of love,*
> *Lee*

A friend told me she saw Lee recently, and there was an
"aliveness" about her. She has become a wonderful testimony to others.

In early New Testament times, people didn't have the
Bible as we know it today to look to. Souls were won to
Christ as Christians went about telling others what God
had done for them. Before He went back to Heaven, Jesus
had said to His disciples: "When the Holy Spirit comes,
you will receive power to go out and tell others what God
has done for you. You will be a witness, running with
your exciting good news" (see Acts 1:8). That was God's
plan for evangelism then, and it is still His plan for evangelism in the twenty-first century.

What I love about these *Effective Prayer Strategies* is that
they teach people how they can connect to God to have
their heartfelt needs met. This allows them to have their
own good news to go out and tell. Answered prayer gives
God glory!

When life throws at us its many and varied circumstances, we can be assured that God has a purpose. He allows situations to be created that will draw us near to Him, so that we can know Him. He is just as hungry for our love and fellowship as we are for His. We were created for this very purpose, to enjoy God and to rest in His presence.

The first prayer page in my *Praying In Your Future* book is "Knowing Jesus." I put this first in the book because it is the ultimate goal of the Gospel. Apostles and prophets are there just to bring us to that place of knowing Him. One reward of learning these prayer strategies is that I now know Him better. I had always hungered for this kind of relationship with the Lord. Speaking the Scriptures not only opened my understanding to know Jesus in a new way, but it has also enabled me to better share with others what He has done for me.

In summary, I find that when we mix abiding in the presence of the Lord with laying claim to the Word of God, we have discovered a powerful mix. Not everyone will pray exactly as I do. Different intercessors have different callings in the realm of prayer, and each of them is good. Each calling has its own purpose, and all of our varied skills mixed together touch the heart of God.

These proven prayer strategies bring us face-to-face with God and enable us to reach out for the Kingdom He has already given to us. It is ours for the taking.

Prayer strategies put me into His presence, and as I behold Him, I am changed from glory to glory:

1. The prayer books are worship books. The promises of the Scriptures are already ours because of the

blood of Jesus. Let us draw near to Him and receive of His hand.

2. Let us laugh for joy over this fact and cling to God with rejoicing.

3. Let God pour His wonderful individual plan and purpose on us.

4. Let Him open doors for our ministries.

5. Let us go through these doors as a mighty army of God.

I laugh with glee, I shout for joy, and my heart melts with awe and thanksgiving when I think of the individual scriptures that have already been fulfilled in my life and in the lives of many others. It is almost too great to ponder, too deep and too high for me to comprehend. I bow before my King in adoration.

Through learning the secrets of *Unlocking the Heavens*, my prayer life has become a great homecoming celebration. I have taken my place in God's Temple and in His courts. I am there because I am a beloved member of His family, and He extends His arms of welcome to you today as well.

Testimonies

I was a little skeptical about the idea of praying prospering scriptures as if I already had the answer and was actually receiving wealth. Maybe other people received money this way, but I was sure I never would. So, first I had to repent of my attitude. Of course the Lord wanted me to prosper.

After applying the principles of praying scriptures as if I already had the answer, checks started arriving in the mail — first $45, and then $98, $160 and $200. Next came a check for $5,800. My husband and I had been working on a business deal for two years, but we felt as if we had been beating our heads against a wall. Then the Lord stepped in and did a miracle, and we saved $34,000 on the transaction. We are not superslick business people, but we do serve an awesome God. He is so good!

* * *

In March of 1996, Ruth put a scripture book together for me and my family. At the time, my son had drifted away from the Lord and was deep into satanic mischief. He was also deeply depressed. My husband was a substance abuser. His dependence on drugs had increased to the point of his using them several times a day. I was at the end of my rope, scared for my loved ones, and I felt abandoned by God.

After applying the principles of praying the Scriptures as if I already had the answer, my family began to change dramatically. My son rededicated his life to the Lord that same month and has been serving Jesus ever since. Two months later, my husband finally ended his twenty-year drug addiction. Three years later, he is still drug-free. Praise the Lord!

* * *

A very hard-working Christian man never seemed to reach his expectations in his job. His long hours of work only brought continual disappointment. His wife was bitter. She would say, "If there is a lousy job to be had, he will find it." He always got what she said.

Then she began to pray the *Prayer Strategy Resource Book,* and to say what God said about her husband. This has turned their lives around. For the past six months, he has been favored and honored at his work, and they will soon be enjoying a free week of vacation in Hawaii, compliments of the company. The company has also supplied him with a new vehicle that he can use for both his family and work and free gasoline for it.

Their son also had many disappointments in life. He had a verbally abusive wife who eventually kicked him out of their home. This past November he married a lovely girl who is like-minded in the ways of God, and who loves him unconditionally. This new daughter-in law has already been a blessing to her in-laws. Last week the son was promoted to management in his company, so that he will be able to support his lovely wife well. He weeps with gratitude in God's presence.

* * *

My Prayer Strategy Resource Book *was published in Russian several months ago. Nina, from the church in Samara, Russia, did the translation. She sent me this testimony:*

When I began to translate the book, I was suffering from a serious nasal problem. I couldn't breathe through my nose without using special medicines. I had been suffering that way for several months. Your strategy seemed to me to be so unusual and strange that I wondered if it could really work. I decided to try it.

I prayed the "Healing" page for two or three days. Then I noticed that I could breathe quite easily. Amazing! This miracle gave me enthusiasm to do the translation work. It was a real pleasure to do it and to discover over and over again how wonderful, loving, rich and generous our Lord is.

* * *

I delved into your prayer strategy books in December, and they are super! I followed your lead, making some adjustments for my six- and seven-year-old grandsons so that they could pray for their mom and dad and themselves. They decorated the pages themselves, and they enjoyed using them to pray.

About two weeks later, their dad (who was backslidden due to some deep hurts in his life) took the family to church for the first time in more than ten years. He went again the next week. There is light in his eyes again, where I had seen only darkness for years.

* * *

A grandmother reports that her granddaughter, who had a personality that seemed to clash with other family members, now is peaceful and friendly, and gets along well with other family members. She is now making wise choices. She is a success. Everyone loves being with her.

* * *

I made up a *Family Prayer Book* for a family and gave copies to the husband, the wife, the wife's sister, and the wife's mother and father. The son in the family had gone through a terrible tragedy. He had been with his best friend when he was killed in a gun accident. He was so affected by the incident that he was unable to finish his senior year in high school because of the emotional impact of the incident.

After the family members started praying the book, however, he was strengthened enough to begin working on getting his GED so that he could pursue a higher education.

A daughter in the family had quit college and gotten married, but now had a desire to go back and get her degree. She says she is happier than ever before, and she and her parents now share a deeper relationship of love and unity.

The husband had been working for a company where he was required to put in long hours and travel a lot, and he had little time for his family. After they began to pray the Scriptures, he was offered a job in a company that likes to see staff members go home at 5 P.M. to be with their families. He also received a good raise and other perks that made his move a blessing. The wife has reported that she now has joy as she shares a new friendship with her husband.

* * *

A wife expressed sorrow because her husband was always putting her down. There was constant discord in the home. She didn't know what to do. I made up a prayer page on "Unity" for her. It was made up of scriptural promises on the Lord breaking down the middle wall of enmity and bringing peace through the cross. We both agreed to pray the page every day.

The next time I saw her, I noticed a change. "You look like things are better with you," I said.

"Yes," she answered, "but not completely."

Soon, however, she began to see a great difference. Her husband became more gentle and less impatient. God is bringing out the most beautiful characteristics in him.

* * *

One woman reported that there had been a big blow up in her family the day she received the book and that she expected a lot of tension in the home that evening. She spent much time praying the "Unity" scriptures the rest of the day. When everyone got home that night, they were all in a good mood — as if nothing had ever happened. What a pleasant surprise that was!

* * *

In September of 1998, Carol got my *Prayer Strategy Resource Book* and began praying the "For Our People" page, which includes Abraham's blessings from Deuteronomy 28 and the promise from Galatians 3:13 that these blessings are now ours because of what Jesus has done for us. I also put this page in the *Praying For Your City* book because I wanted these prayers to cause the Christians of our cities to bloom and flourish, coming forth with a testimony.

Carol was drawn to the paraphrased part that said, "My grocery sacks are full, and so are my cupboards." Another phrase that blessed her was, "Everything I set my hand to is blessed." Daily, she would read the page over and over.

One day, some neighbor children were at her house and she was feeding them snacks. Just then, her friend Debbie stopped over. When Debbie saw what Carol was doing, she asked, "How can you afford to feed these children?" She was helping to pass out food for a ministry called Changing Our City, and she suggested that Carol could possibly get leftovers from them to feed the neighborhood children. Carol met with leaders of the Changing Our City ministry, and they suggested she also give food to the families of the children she had been feeding.

Debbie helped her, and as they would pass out the food, they would add a prayer page from the *Prayer Strategy Resource Book*. Soon the neighbors were asking for prayer for their needs.

Others helped Carol as well. Norm, for instance, volunteered to drive his truck and pick up the food. He also donated the pamphlets "Starting Over" and "Knowing God."

Carol's ministry has now expanded to seven trailer courts, and many other volunteers are helping her with their time. One of those volunteers, Rev. Darrell, has become her husband.

Is there a prayer page for getting a godly husband? Yes, someone made over the "Pastors" page and put in "Husband" where it said "Pastor." Carol said that everything she had wanted in a husband was on that "Pastor" page, and after beginning to pray those promises, she had her man.

* * *

In the fall of 1998, a Methodist pastor from Indianapolis invited me to his church to see how he could implement the prayer books for his staff. We took pages out of the *Prayer Strategy Resource Book* so they would have a different topic for each day.

When I saw him in July, he told me he had never handed out the books. Because he had such a burden for the lost, however, he had made copies of "The Lost" and "Pastor" pages and had given them to ten women to pray as a test. Since that time, his attendance had doubled, and they had been forced to have two services on Sunday. They have hired a Christian education director. Before, they had only five children in the third to fifth grade Sunday school class, and now they had between fifty and sixty every Sunday.

It all happened in a very strange way. The pastor's first-grade daughter invited friends from her class to an Easter egg hunt the church was having. Out of that, many families from the PTA began attending the church and giving their lives to the Lord. These were "The Lost" for whom they had been praying.

The church didn't have a program of evangelism, but people were just walking into the church and getting saved. The anointing on the pastor had risen, but he recognized that it was not anything he was doing personally. God was at work.

*   *   *

A woman stopped by my house to say that someone had given her a *Praying For Your City* book. Her son had been deep in sin for many years. When she started praying the book (designed to help win others to the Lord), her own son was wonderfully saved and was now on fire for the Lord.

*   *   *

These past several years, since praying the "Pastor" page for the pastors of our city, we notice that God has been bringing in new pastors who have a heart for prayer and revival for our city.

*   *   *

A single mom realized she needed divine help with raising her children, so she began to speak forth the promise of a scripture on the "Family" page. She would say, "My children are growing in wisdom and stature and in favor with God and man." As the years went by, she often prayed this prayer throughout the day, rejoicing as she did it. God wonderfully answered her, for her children are beautiful examples for all to see. They receive favor and honor wherever they go.

One of her children was not easy to get along with, but because of this promise and her action on it, he turned into a good example for all to see, winning top honors in his Christian school for his good character and spiritual ways.

* * *

One autumn, I spoke to a prayer group in South Bend, Indiana. Afterward, they would look through my book for one or two scriptural prayers for each concern, and would pray that for the following week. The next spring, they sent me a letter telling me about God's answers. One of their stories was about four people who had an alcohol problem, who were now recovering. Three divorced mothers regained and/or retained visitation privileges and custody of their children. Two persons had obtained jobs or promotions.

Praying Psalm 118:16-17 had enabled three people to successfully face bone marrow transplants, two to face heart surgery and another to survive pneumonia complicated by heart problems. Using Deuteronomy 28:4 has resulted in seeing the delivery of seven healthy babies (one set of twins). Three of the pregnancies were fraught with difficulties (bleeding problems, dehydration, premature labor and the potential for Down's syndrome) and involved much medical intervention. All the babies are perfect and beautiful.

* * *

I spoke in a church in Muncie, Indiana, and a woman who had been suffering depression for years bought my *Prayer Strategy Resource Book*. Her mind was so troubled that she began to pray the book, just to keep her mind focused and away from her confused thoughts. She continued this steadily for a whole week. Toward the end of the week, the Spirit of the Lord came upon her and set her free from depression. That Sunday, she shared at church, and the Lord came down on the whole congregation. People were moved to rush to the altar.

* * *

OTHER BOOKS

Prayer Strategy Resource Book

This book has an individual topic for each page, so a person can pick out prayer pages that fit their need or desire. Jesus has already won it all for them. He is waiting bless to them in an individual way. It is a 81/2 11, 80 page book. And also smaller size, same book 5.5 x 8.

Praying In Your Future

Let God unfold the future He has planned for you. Prayer focus for each day of the week, or you can pray the whole book, or pick and choose what you want. It is a 5x7 , 32 page Pamphlet

Miracle Family Prayer Book (51/2x81/2, 32 page pamphlet)

Has a page a day to pray for building strong families, that all in family can pray in agreement with. Tittles: Forgiving and Blessing, Unity (perhaps the most powerful page in the book), Father, Mother, Children, Family, Prosper, God's Love For Me.

Praying For Your City (51/2x81/2, 32 page pamphlet)

A prayer page for each day. When people agree in prayer, great things happen. People washing their city with the blessings of redemption of the cross.

Fear Not 4x51/2, 20 page pamphlet)

Jewish prayer book, to calm our spirits with scriptures from the Old Testament that wash us with God's faithfulness.

For Israel- We Declare God's Word Praying the promises for Israel to spring forth into God's plan and blessings.

Scriptural Prayers With Music The two cassettes below combined on a CD. My sons, Tom and Dave Shinness, did the music and I say the Prayers. Let us know how you like them.
Living Waters Dave on clarinet, Tom on guitar. cassette
Praying In Your Future Tom on guitar. cassette

Unlocking The Heavens Seminar DVD Ruth's Testimony, of going from defeat and discouragement's to being a winner. Four hour Seminar.

CD's by Tom Shinness

Translucent Harp (instrumental) featuring the Gibson's
 Harp guitar, plus many other strings - all Tom.
Many Waters full of instruments blending, -awesome.
 Canadian Musician Magazine interviewing a writer several
 months ago asked "What is the hottest thing going on in
 Nashville today?" and he replied "Tom Shinness."